Embracing the Magic of NOW

As Kye Crow fell to the ground, clutching her face, feeling sick and dizzy and full of fear, she soon realised Kunkaa, her Camel had given her a big wake up call.

by Kye Crowe

It was getting late in the day and my partner Gill and I had been unable to find a decent place with plenty of feed for our animals, to pull up and camp. We were travelling through the desert in a wagon, pulled by eight camels and altogether, we had over fifty rescued animals travelling with us - goats, dogs, donkey, parrots, pigeons and chickens too.

I was exhausted and stressed. We had only been travelling a week, and some days, despite giving it everything we had, we barely made it a kilometre down the road. Nothing was flowing as expected and caring for all these animals as we travelled was really hard work! I felt deeply let down. We had been guided by Spirit to leave on this journey. To let go of our newly renovated home, our possessions, and trust. I had struggled to let go. How could I trust such crazy guidance? We had even let go of having a destination! All we knew was we would be guided to the perfect place to create a sanctuary for all the animals that needed our help. I was so excited at the prospect of our sanctuary, I couldn't wait to be there and I was irritated and impatient at every delay.

I was leading our camel Kunkaa, which means crow in Pitjantjatjara. Crow has always taught me to find the gifts in our shadows, so it's very symbolic it was this camel that taught me such a huge lesson.

I was so frustrated. I thought our journey would take a month or two, and then we could settle back down into domestic bliss at our dreamt-of sanctuary. I was so distracted that I was unprepared when Kunkaa jumped up and clouted me with her front foot, full force on my face.

I fell on the ground, clutching my face, feeling sick and dizzy and full of fear. I had no idea what damage that kick had done. Gill, my partner ran over with ice from our solar fridge and made me lay in the shade whilst he settled all the animals and tethered them out for the night.

Fortunately, although I was badly shaken, my face was only bruised. This event was a huge wake up call. I sat up late that night, my back against a beautiful She Oak tree whose trailing feathery leaves whispered in the breeze. It was a full moon, and for the first time I felt present in my body. I was not thinking about the past or dreaming of the future. That kick had landed me right in the NOW. I was shocked at how out of my body I'd been. How could I even hope to work with these animals safely if I wasn't even present! I was so grateful for that kick. It had been a brutal awakening, but with all these animals, it could have been a lot worse!

I realised then that I had left on this trip with all these expectations of progress and success, as if I was running a business. If we didn't travel twenty kilometres each day, we had failed. I had left no room for the magic to unfold. I was so focused on my destination I had failed to enjoy the moment.

Our trip ended up taking us three years and we travelled over 2,200 kilometres. I learnt the only way we could be guided was if we let go of everything, even our expectations of how things should be. If we felt like chatting all day to someone we met on the side of the road, we would. If we felt like camping for a week, we did and when we got stuck in mud up to our wagon's axle, we trusted there was a reason. There was! The kind farmer that pulled us out showed us a much better route than the one we were on. Even our adversities became gifts, when we remained open!

Whilst I'm still passionate about creating and building our sanctuary, all our animals constantly remind me to stay centred and present in the now, and in this sacred space, everything unfolds - magically, harmoniously and joyfully.

Whilst I have always been driven to make this world a better place, how I do that is much simpler now. I'm not aiming for something outside of myself. The sanctuary I create is within. Everything begins with me. Right here, right now. Letting go in love.

Kye Crow is the Creatress of Wunjo Crow, a range of Goddess clothing that's sprinkled with love and sewn with magic. Kye and her partner Gill live with over a 100 rescued animals and teach Sacred Journeys into the Animal Realms, the power of Love and how to live on planet earth as a sensitive. Contact Kye at: Web: www.camelcampsanctuary.com Facebook: www.facebook.com/Wunjocrow Photo Credit: Argnesh Rose Visionary Digital Artist specialising in fantasy and totem portraiture – Web: www.givethemwings.com.au

Your Soul's Purpose

Reveal your Soul's Purpose with this Daily Soul Conversation from Kerrie Wearing

The Soul, your Soul, arises from the most powerful of creations where nothing exists without intention and purpose. Therefore it only stands to reason that your Soul, having been born from that source - the powerful creator - would also have an intention and purpose for existing, would it not?

This intention and purpose is what I term your Soul's purpose. Each of us are born with an intention for the Soul to evolve into the best expression of itself that it can be. How it chooses to execute this intention through a set of individual life circumstances and experiences is the very fabric of why each of us are so different. And what is so amazing to me is the fact that each of us have an Ego and a Spirit perfectly suited to support the task and purpose. We are all Spirit housed within the Soul, along with our ego, and all magically and perfectly designed to live out the reason and life you were born to live.

Your Spirit is the guiding force, the Soul's compass if you will, keeping you on track and in alignment with your Soul's evolutionary intention and pre-birth plan. This occurs, whether we realize it or not, when moments of Destiny are employed to try and help us engage or re-align with this pathway. Any moment in life that leads us to deconstruct ourselves and our life is one of those moments trying to steer us closer to our Spirit and its Soul purpose. Whether it is relationship breakdowns, health scares or the loss of a loved one, many forms of grief are destined to play their part in waking us into awareness, as was the case for one of my clients recently.

Angela's husband had passed away a couple of years ago, leaving her with two young children to raise. This experience had already woken the Spirit within Angela, though she still had many questions as to why he would leave. When I communicated that her husband was explaining this was part of their Soul agreement, that his purpose for being here was to give Angela the gift of awakening her Spirit by leaving, Angela knew and felt this within her own Soul to be true. Knowing this then allowed Angela a little more healing, giving her a new feeling of peace and a sense of being able to go forward and allowing herself to be happy. Then, with further confirmation coming for Angela in the days that followed, Angela knew her husband was and would always be here to help her evolve and grow.

Awakening into awareness is the first step to not only live from the Soul, but to consciously discover what your Soul purpose is. We must fully understand we are Spirit within a Soul first and foremost, if we are to fully appreciate how this affects our human experience, and therefore to be able to live the fullest expression of who we are meant to be. Or, in real terms, live consciously aligned to our Soul purpose as much as we can within the limitation of this modern world.

At this point I'd like to differentiate that your Soul purpose is not always inexplicably linked or is the same as your life purpose. For some people they will be totally connected, but not all. For example, one of the most common Soul purposes I come across in my work as a Soul coach is the Soul's intention to evolve through people's relationships.

> *Awakening into awareness is the first step to not only live from the Soul, but to consciously discover what your Soul purpose is.*

The Australian Afterlife Explorers Conference

PARRAMATTA RSL
SYDNEY, AUSTRALIA
Jan 24th – 26th 2015
9.30am – 6.00pm daily

Death is one of life's greatest mysteries. Do we really die, or do we have a soul that lives on apart from the body? Join us at the Australian Afterlife Explorers Conference to discover and explore, through western science and spirituality, fascinating knowledge and evidence relating to the progression of the soul and the continuity of consciousness after physical death.

Barry Eaton
Uncovering the Secrets of Life after Death

Ezio & Michelle De Angelis
Postcards from the Other Side –
A Spirit's Guide to the Afterlife

Karina Machado
The Power of Love: The Transformative Effects of After-Death Contact

Val Hood
The Important Work of Spirit Guides and Transitioned Souls

Adam Rock
Mediumship: The Survival Hypothesis

Scott Podmore
Conversations with Mediums

Glennys Mackay
Wayward Spirits and Earthbound Souls

Trisha McCagh
Animal Insights into the Afterlife

Christine Morgan
The Hidden Meaning of the Spirit

Allen Tiller
Modern Technology and Spirit Communication

Debbie Malone
How My Near Death Experiences Transformed My Life

Victor Zammit
The Greatest Evidence for the Afterlife

Peter Smith
Life Between Lives - Awakening an Understanding of Your Immortal Identity & Quantum Consciousness – Expanding your Personal Universe

Michael Roads
The Metaphysical Experiences of Following and Observing Three Souls at the Moment of Physical Death

Rob Smith
Anomalous Voices, Multidimensional Communication, and the Continuity of Consciousness...

Michele Knight
A New Way of Being in the World: Findings From a Doctoral Research Study Exploring After-death Contact

Alexandra Browne-Hill
Loving Intuition on the Ground Floor

Natasha Tassell
NDEs and Consciousness

Mary Murray
Precognitive Dreams about Death and Dying and the Nature of Consciousness

Joe Vandermeer
The Profound Implications of the Near-Death and Similar Experiences

Only 300 seats available each day so reserve yours now at:
WWW.AFTERLIFEEXPLORERS.COM.AU

Note : Speakers, Subjects & Timetable subject to change without notice

Editor's Note

Each Soul is born into this life with a specific intention to evolve and grow into love and wisdom, and yet the Soul is wise enough to know how best to achieve this.

Through a set of life circumstances designed to support a specific evolutionary goal, your Soul purpose incorporates an awareness of the collective evolutionary goal while fine tuning the growth of the individual. While often thought of as one's life's purpose and what one may make their life's work, in truth they are often connected, but not always. And while every living being has a Soul purpose, not every person may be walking the path their Soul intended for this life.

And so it is with this issue of inSpirit Magazine we seek to provide you, our fellow Soul traveler, with a range of inSights, articles and tools around this very topic. I, myself share a Soul Conversation designed to engage your Spirit into revealing your Soul purpose. New York Times best-selling author Gabrielle Bernstein shares with you her Top 5 tips to discover one's Soul purpose in life. And Nicola McIntosh delves into the Soul purpose of Nature.

We bid farewell to Brendan D Murphy, who has been a wealth of information on Science and Spirituality, this edition. Thank you Brendan for your time, energy and support, and we all wish you every success with your future projects.

It is with much excitement that we welcome on board this issue Scott Alexander King. Scott is a shaman, visionary and Zoomancer, bringing a wealth of knowledge and life experience to his new Spirited Animalia column. We are very blessed to have Scott as a member of the inSpirit team.

This issue facilitated a range of articles inspired by some of the team's very personal and heartfelt journeys to discover their own truth and soul purposes. Perhaps something that is said helps you to see how your Soul purpose is flowing through your life, and how it connects you to others, or even inspires you to commit to discovering what your Soul purpose truly is.

With love & gratitude, Kerrie

THE TEAM

MANAGING EDITOR Kerrie Wearing

CREATIVE TEAM Kerrie Wearing, Nicolle Poll, Alex Cayas, Therese Chesworth

EDITOR Nicolle Poll, Therese Chesworth

REGULAR CONTRIBUTORS Kerrie Wearing, Nicolle Poll, Nicola McIntosh, Susanne Hartas, Jude Garracht Gem~mer, Meadow Linn, Alex Cayas, Natasha Heard, Laura Naomi, Kye Crow, Reilly McCarron, Rita Maher, Amanda Coppa, Nicole Humber, Scott Alexander King, Toni Reilly

GUEST CONTRIBUTORS Gabrielle Bernstein

GRAPHIC DESIGN Kerrie Wearing, Nicola McIntosh

COVER ARTWORK Nicolle Poll

Produced by Kerrie Wearing and inSpirit Publishing, inSpirit Magazine is designed to provide a respectful forum for like-minded souls to share in a community which aims to provide informative views, opinions and education regarding the experience of living with Spirit. Disclaimer: While every care has been taken to provide the reader with accurate, inSpiring and thought-provoking information, the Publishers take no responsibility for the accuracy of information and views expressed by the Contributors. The views and opinions expressed by contributors are not necessarily shared by the Editor Publishers.

In This Issue

4 Your Soul's Purpose

3 Embracing the Magic of NOW
6 Past Lives and Soul Purpose
8 From the Pond to the Palace
10 The Lost and Forgotten Ones
12 Nature's Soul Purpose
14 Your Top 5 tips to Discover One's Soul Purpose in Life
16 The Inherent Soul Agreement
18 Seeking a Magical Name
19 Sacred Snake Shifting
22 Because We All Agreed
23 Soul Purpose Salad
24 Birth is the New Beginning
25 Soul Song

Regular Columns

11 Buddhism
11 For the Love of Angels
13 Crystal Q & A
19 Goddess inSpiration
20 Spirited Animalia
21 Cosmic Codes
27 inSpirit Reviews
28 inSpirit Directory

23

25

14

20

This Soul purpose often presents with challenging relationships and it is not uncommon to find these people with multiple life partners, estranged family members or even long periods of trying to find love. This Soul purpose does not hinge entirely on what it is you choose to do for work or a career. Aside from providing an environment for which this Soul is to meet people who need to be in their life, the type of work is not a significant driving factor for evolution. However, choosing to focus on your passions and what you love doing will bring often the strength and JOY you need to live a Soul purpose such as this. Even if we look briefly at Angela's husband, his Soul purpose was to be here for Angela, to serve her in a way that only he could. Therefore what he did for work, or how he contributed to this world, were rudimentary compared to his true Soul purpose and being a catalyst for Angela's spiritual awakening.

Aligning consciously with your Soul's purpose is far simpler than we perceive. This flows naturally for many of us, and certainly, for those of you who give your Spirit within a daily voice, you will find meeting your Soul's purpose inevitable. There is, however, much to be said about living your Soul's purpose with conscious awareness. Allowing yourself to live with the knowing there is a real purpose for your existence is the most empowering gift you can give yourself.

You will find life takes on a flow of ease and grace as you come to accept life and how it is meant to be, because you know it is all perfectly designed to support your Soul purpose.

If there is one tool I can offer you to support you in aligning more closely with your Soul purpose, it is this simple daily Soul Conversation. Taken from my new 'Wisdom of the Soul; Daily Soul Conversation' insight deck, use this question each morning as you wake but before you get out of bed. If it helps, hold your hand over your heart to help focus your awareness, and then without thinking, accept the thought, feeling or vision which comes to mind. Even if at first you feel that what you think you are receiving is not real, please persist. Your Spirit and Soul knows what you are working towards by giving it this voice. In time the process will transcend and you will hear from the Divine Spirit within.

Daily Soul Conversation: My Soul says, to move me forward to understanding my true Soul purpose, I need to…..

Lastly, it is important that you action any direction that was given. If you need to 'Be' then just 'Be'. If you need to make hard decisions, then know that in time this does need to be done. No matter what is called for, it is the following through and taking action that actually moves you closer to your Soul purpose and being your true self.

Kerrie Wearing is an internationally recognised Soul Coach and Medium, specialising in coaching and mentoring people to connect with their unique Soul Purpose. She is the author of A New Kind of Normal; Unlock the Medium Within, managing editor of inSpirit Magazine and director of inSpirit Publishing. Website: www.kerriewearing.com

PAST LIVES AND SOUL PURPOSE

PAST LIFE FACILITATOR AND TRAINER, TONI REILLY REVEALS HOW HER OWN PAST LIFE EXPERIENCE SET THE WHEELS IN MOTION TO DISCOVERING HER SOUL PURPOSE

Why am I here? What is my purpose? Am I on path? At some stage we ponder these questions and at that point our lives take a turn, a positive turn towards seeking deeper meaning to our existence. It's called soul-searching.

For me this stage may have subconsciously always been a question, however I did not take much notice or seriously ponder my existence until I was around 30 years old. That is when I began to ask myself what my life was all about. There were insecurities which I had around body image which dissolved at that age because I felt more at peace with myself and much more grateful for the wonderful things in my life. I had three lovely, healthy children, I had a husband who loved me and I thought my life was full. God knows time wise I could not have fit much more in as my days were filled with work and taking care of three small children.

Thinking about myself or what I wanted to do really was not up for discussion as I was a mother and my husband's work was most important. Isn't that the way it is? Surely my life must have purpose? I used to have regular thoughts as a teenager, about the time I started working, that I was to help people. This seemed strange to me as I was a shop assistant and the only help I gave was in the form of 'service with a smile'.

Around the time I was 32 I questioned my life even more. I felt oppressed in my marriage, the things that I wanted to do were not possible due to commitments to my children and my husband's work being the priority. Occasionally I would find a course scheduled on the weekend, but even those did not eventuate, as he had to work the weekend. There was no compromise and I never realised I was valuable enough to insist on the importance of me attending.

I began to question my relationship, I wondered if there was more to life than running around, cleaning, working to make ends meet, taking care of children and a partner. Surely there was?

In 2006 I travelled to Egypt, which was something I felt I wanted to do since I was small. I hijacked a friend's travel plans and went. That trip was the beginning of major realisations for me. I did not consider myself spiritual then, nor did I find Egypt or the Pyramids to be particularly powerful energy wise. For me, they seemed raped of their energies because the people had to survive one way or another and so bribery and corruption were rife. What transpired on my trip was a realisation of how little material things mattered. Possessions, which were so valued in Western culture, actually meant nothing. It was people who mattered. It was as though my rose coloured glasses came off. The media, for example, was so clearly contrived to control people with fear, and this is when I stopped watching television.

I wanted more for my life. I wanted to do 'something' and I still had no idea what that was. First I wanted my freedom, in the sense that I wanted to be able to live day to day not worrying about what my partner thought of me and what his reaction might be. I was lonely. I felt isolated. I did all this to myself - all I had to do was speak up. I did not, I could not. I never wanted to rock the boat or make anyone feel bad because of me. Because I rarely if ever spoke up, lost control or asked for help, I had painted this unrealistic picture of our life. Everyone thought we had a perfect marriage. I never told anyone that I used to cry on the couch all by myself most nights.

This oppression became intense. I was very aware that I had caused all of this - that my partner had not forced me to feel the way I did, he had not told me to keep my feelings to myself. On the contrary - if there was a rare time that I would say what was wrong, he would make efforts to support me. I lived with the silent treatment for a great portion of our 16 years together. I always thought the silence and withdrawal happened because of me. I must have done something, but what? I felt hard done by, I felt sorry for myself, I justified to myself that I was a good person; I did not deserve to be 'in trouble'. In hindsight, I know that I was not the cause of the 'silent treatment' nor did I need to take everything personally, but that is all part of my personal growth.

Now I understand where insecurity fits into our psyche and the reactions and behaviours that we develop and continue to act out until the time that we wake up. Waking up is the result of soul-searching. It is so powerful, and life is never the same once this epiphany is reached.

That is not to say that there were no more challenges in life - on the contrary for me. I really thought I did not have any issues. Once I started looking at myself, meditating week after week, there was more stuff - so much that I wondered how much can there possibly be? There was so much! Where had all these issues come from? Why now?

Around the time I was 36 my life took a huge change in direction. I left my marriage, and began to study and nurture my sixth senses, which were apparently innate in me. It was also at this stage that I was introduced to the Brian Weiss book *'Many Lives, Many Masters'.* This book changed my life. Everything I read made me feel comfort - I knew it was true. His words, the experiences, the cases all resonated at my core and I knew that past lives were to be at least a part of my life purpose.

This is when my awakening quickened. It was as though my life prior to this barely existed. But it did, and I was in emotional turmoil over the loss of my marriage for years, but I still soldiered on. I was on a mission. I was not sure exactly what that mission was but somehow it fitted with my teenage thoughts of 'helping people'. So cliché, I know, but that is what happened. I had direction. I had to unravel myself, layer by layer and bare my soul to the world so that they could see how people are, to know that we are not alone and nor are we that different to other people.

I first experienced my own past life memories with the lady who told me to read that book. I had specific weird issues that I asked to find out about during my session. Sure enough, they were addressed and my experience assured me of the power of people rummaging through past lives to discover themselves, their capabilities, their power, their value, and their purpose. My life took off - that is the only way I can express that stage. It was as though I was free and liberated. I still kept most of my personal realisations to myself. I was not prepared to be vulnerable to ridicule, and I felt as though no one would understand.

Life purpose is different for each of us, but the same in some ways. The things we are here to learn are similar and ultimately strive towards the same outcome, which is tolerance and acceptance of each other and ourselves.

One thing I can assure you is that you are never off track, and when the going gets tough, it does not mean that you are off path. On the contrary, difficult circumstances are the reason we grow, they are part of our purpose. As humans, we never realise this until hindsight. If we could see clearly the purpose of tragedy and hurtful experiences, we would not live through them, we would know to sidestep. Even if we can see other people's paths clearly, we can never see our own as we are too invested in the outcome.

Live your life, value all of your experiences, positive and challenging, as they all contribute to your soul's purpose.

Toni Reilly is an internationally recognised Past Life facilitator and professional trainer. After training with Dr. Brian Weiss she devised her own unique techniques. As the founder of Toni Reilly Institute she developed the Diploma of SoulLife™ Psychology, a professional qualification for intuitive practitioners. www.tonireillyinstitute.com | www.tonireilly.com.au | info@tonireilly.com.au |

+ 61 0413 088 970

Photo Credit: Tina Fiveash www.tinafiveash.com.au

From the Pond to the Palace

Reilly McCarron shares with you how life, transformation and listening to the Soul can lead you to very your own personal palace of dreams.

> *Sometimes our intuition, our bodies, or our dreams tell us when we're on the right (or wrong) path.*

Ben, my husband, sometimes jokes that he is a lost descendent of the Romanov dynasty. Despite the realities of our modest circumstances, Ben quips that he belongs to the aristocracy; that his true calling is to join the idle rich. He jests, to a degree, but there's some truth in his self-appraisal. Regardless of financial wealth and titles, Ben is as noble, kind, handsome and charming as any Romanov (or Disney) prince.

Who are we, really? Can you remember what you're here for? It's a loaded question suggesting there's a reason you are who you are in this time and place. Shakespeare wrote 'to thine own self be true', yet this assumes we know ourselves well enough to do so. And while quiet contemplation can bring insights into the Self, it's often through the trials and tribulations, the wonders and delights of day-to-day living that we come to better know ourselves, and each other.

Sometimes our intuition, our bodies, or our dreams tell us when we're on the right (or wrong) path. We may hear an inner voice whispering 'this way' and 'that way' and 'sit here awhile and listen'. Recognising and following our Soul purpose can be difficult, but well worth the effort when

the windows start lining up and the soulshine pours in to rejuvenate our weary hearts. When we recognise the markings along our unique path, we are wise to pay heed, even when others around us are flowing in a different direction.

During my career in the television industry, I became a storyteller, played harp, and studied folklore and fairy tales in my spare time, thinking I might somehow weave these threads together after retiring. In 2010 the ABC made my position redundant and it seemed 'retirement' had come earlier than expected. While I didn't feel altogether ready, I decided to follow my alternate path and started a small business which brought together my passions. I researched fairy tales overseas, wrote a show and toured it interstate, presented at conferences, wrote articles, and co-founded the Australian Fairy Tale Society, all without much apparent effort on my part. Rather than struggling to get these things off the ground it felt more like riding a wave.

Having recently become a mum, I have now wound down faerie bard to focus on my darling boy, and am thrilled to discover all those skills have found their true place in my life. What a delight it is to sing, tell stories, play harp, and play games with my baby son! I might have chosen to ignore my soulful yearnings for such frivolous pastimes as playing harp, spinning wool, and telling tales, but my soul would have gone hungry, and starvation of the soul is not something I wish to teach my child. By following the signs along my true path I have filled my basket with nourishment, softened my heart with nurturance, and found my way to the refreshing spring of creativity.

There are many enchanted transformations in fairy tales, and one that beautifully describes a soul on his true path is The Frog Prince (also known as The Princess and the Frog). The frog, knowing himself to be an enchanted Prince, sees his match in the Princess and strikes a deal with her - he will retrieve her beloved golden ball from the pond if she accepts his companionship. She agrees but quickly wishes to break their deal. He holds the Princess to her word, and squelches his way ever closer to her, until she throws him at a wall in disgust. In this moment the enchantment is broken and he becomes a Prince once more. (In American versions she kisses the frog.) This little froggy knew his true destiny and acted patiently and honourably to claim it.

If you believe your Soul has a purpose here but you're not sure what it is, asking with an open heart might be enough to remind you. Trusting your intuition may lead you down unexpected paths, away from the village and into the woods, where you find your inner Self waiting patiently, ready to guide you along your soul path to the palace of your dreams.

Reilly McCarron is the creator and enchantress of 'faerie bard', and President of the Australian Fairy Tale Society. She is a singer/songwriter, a Bard with the Order of Bards, Ovates and Druids (OBOD), an accredited member of the Australian Storytelling Guild (NSW) and has a Graduate Diploma in Australian Folklore with a particular interest in fairy tales.

Contact Reilly at: Email: austfairytales@gmail.com Web: www.facebook.com/austfairytales

The Lost and Forgotten Ones

Gem Green reveals the soul secrets of the Sea Goddess of the Lost and Forgotten Ones

As the soul speaks, we listen. We are motivated pioneers, travellers, explorers and discoverers when it comes to seeking out the messages, the purpose, the agreements of the soul.

For the most part we are eager and willing to participate in this journey of discovering the true soul of the self. And, for the most part, we are eager and willing to share our soul journeys with others, to accept others for what they are here to do and we often do so lovingly and compassionately.

Yet there is another side to this discovery of the soul's truth, one that is a little darker, a little forgotten and even a little ignored. I speak of the ones whom we tend not to see beyond the surface. I speak of the souls that willingly or unwillingly, refuse to enter into the realms of their soul truth. I speak of those ones that, for one reason or another, have been lost as if swallowed by the depths of the ocean and long forgotten by the sands of time. I speak of the lost and forgotten ones.

The lost and forgotten ones are bountiful and the reasons plentiful also. Yet there is one I can share with you. Of those who light the way for those who are lost and forgotten, there is one who can be counted on to gather those that are lost and those that are forgotten. There is one who recognises these souls before they themselves recognise the plights of their soul stories, their purpose. And, there is one who recognises this above and before everyone else.

She is the Sea Goddess of The Lost and Forgotten Ones.

Those who become lost and or forgotten, have journeyed through their lifetime detached from the true essence of their soul, blindly or compliantly, it does not matter as each is as irrelevant as the other when the result is always the same; seekers and wanderers of the essence of the soul, the meaning of it all and the purpose they were to fulfil upon the earthly realms, now long forgotten and left swimming in a sea of confusion. The Sea Goddess of The Lost and Forgotten Ones is a shining beacon for those who have passed without knowing the truth of their soul selves, gathering in all the lost and the forgotten, holding them to her sea soaked bosom, comforting and guiding them through to the next stage of their existence as gently and as gracefully as she can.

Yet she also encompasses the very essence of soul discovery as she reaches in, connects and guides her light to the recesses, the caverns, the sea trenches of those in the living that have lost and/or forgotten the journey their soul selves agreed upon before breathing their first breath of life on this earthly plane. She is a sea soul spirit ready and willing to help you find your way when it comes to discovering the deep and powerful agreement of the soul. And, she will guide you to operating from your true and authentic soul self well after you have remembered your truth.

The Sea Goddess of The Lost and Forgotten Ones is as old as the first soul to draw breath in the physical realms - she is as ancient as time itself. Healing wisdom of ancient times and soul connections course through her waterlogged veins. Her wild nature is raw and real, and she will peel away, she will draw you out and she will set you free.

---

*Connect and draw yourself into the grid of the Sea Goddess of the Lost and Forgotten Ones to reveal your truth or quietly recite the chant below to call upon her for guidance and assistance.

Drawn into the depths by a stranger, deep into the darkness of the abyss.

Drawn into the depths by a stranger, the currents and tides are changing.

Drawn into the depths by a stranger, one who has my heart wrapped up.

Drawn into the depths by a stranger, the light upon her being beginning to glow.

Drawn into the depths by a stranger, the words floating and flowing like magick.

Drawn into the depths by a stranger, the heart opening, revealing and flowing.

Drawn into the depths by a stranger, the 'knowing' and awareness returning like a friend.

Drawn into the depths by a stranger, to reveal the true soul purpose of my eternal being.

Drawn into the depths by my long lost friend, once forgotten, now remembered, for all of time.

Gem embraces the energetic power of seashells, sea animals and the waters of ocean and sea every day, connecting and creating with this amazing and unique energy to enhance and guide not only her magickal life journey but yours as well if you allow it. "May The Magick & Wisdom of Ocean & Sea's Inspire Us All" www.gemgreen.com.au

Be Mindful

By Radnamaya

In spirituality, we emphasise a lot on the importance of interdependence, which is of course based on the universal law of Karma. As human beings, we always think that we are the smartest, we are the most experienced and we have the most right and the top priority when it comes to the ownership of the world and the Earth's resources. There is a saying "absolute power corrupts absolutely". Because we humans feel that we are the absolute owner of the Earth, therefore gradually we start to take it for granted and to abuse it, sometimes knowingly, sometimes unconsciously. When we suffer the negative consequences, we normally forget that we planted the seeds of these consequences. So we blame our suffering on everyone else, even on the divine, without having a good reflection on our own deeds, on what we have done.

We are the creator of our own sorrows and our own happiness. So it's better to start to be mindful and bring a 'Karmic mirror' with us all the time, so that before we blame our failures on others, let's take out this mirror and have a good reflection - "What did I do before, now that I am now suffering?" This analytical understanding will at least help us not to continue to make the same mistakes or the same decisions, and encourage us to always be mindful of our intentions, our thoughts and our actions.

What I am trying to say is, since we consider humans, ourselves, to be more intelligent, we should also try our best to be more understanding and appreciate. Understanding in the sense that we are all sharing the same home, and we should try to respect other beings, to protect nature and to live in harmony with nature. We want to live safely and happily, without worries, but we are not creating this environment nor the conditions, yet we keep on blaming others for our unhappiness. This doesn't make sense for any intelligent mind.

Words written by my Guru from Jigme Radnamaya

Words inspired by my Guru from Radnamaya.
You can contact Radnamaya by email: radnamaya@live.com

For the love of Angels

By Suzanne Hartas

THE ANGEL SAYS: DEAR ONES, EACH AND EVERY ONE OF YOU ARE PART OF A UNIVERSAL CONSCIOUSNESS AND HAVE BEEN CREATED AS INDIVIDUAL ASPECTS FROM THE ONE ETERNAL LIGHT. SEPARATION FROM GOD IS MERELY AN ILLUSION, FOR YOU ARE BORN OF THE ETERNAL LIGHT AND SO IT IS FROM NOW UNTIL ETERNITY.

Every soul has a 'Divine Blueprint', created from the one Divine light. Your soul has an energy and vibration unique unto yourself, yet you are still part of the Oneness. As individual aspects of the source consciousness, the divine qualities of every soul are an integral part of the completion of the whole, for the purpose of your creation is to remember your God self, then return home and merge once again with the Oneness.

You are the journeyman, Dear Ones, living many lifetimes in human form, seeking to evolve in love through experience, and ultimately dissolving the illusion of separation from the Divine. Before your incarnation, with the guidance and support of your guides, angels and soul family, a divine script for your life was created, in which your soul family, with whom you have shared many lifetimes, will assist you in achieving your soul's intended goals. They have agreed to play the role of your mirror, reflecting back to you the areas in which your soul requires growth and this growth will be evident through the quality and purity of the love you have for one self.

While every soul has a unique divine script, the journey of all souls are interwoven and interconnected within the Creator's greater script of the 'Divine Plan'. For it is indeed a journey of evolution for the collective of souls, which you cannot experience without the experience of another. We understand your awareness of your soul's eternal self may seem hidden from your view, but know this, Beloved Ones, you carry the light of your soul within your heart, and it is through the doorway of your heart that the glow of your eternal consciousness will radiate forth like a beacon, navigating you toward the truth of your perfection once again. Much love.

Susanne Hartas is a Psychic Medium and Angel Intuitive.

Please contact Suzanne at: *www.inspiritmagazine.com; mail@inspiritmagazine.com*

Nature's Soul Purpose

'Every living being on this planet has a soul purpose'

We each have a purpose. Every living thing on this planet has a soul purpose. It is easy to think that Humans' purposes have more importance, because we are under the false impression that we are the most intelligent species. To date we believe we haven't found a comparable intelligent life-form, so we keep searching for its existence. As long as we continue to believe we are separate from everything around us, we will continue on this path.

Everything is energy. In fact everything is vibration. Every living object, every living thing on the planet, is just energy vibrating at different rates. We are not really a solid form, but because this is the limit of our thinking and the limit to what our five senses tell us, this is why we create the limitation that we are separate from everything.

When we start to open our minds to new concepts, we allow other possibilities to enter our belief structure and this can lead to a very big awakening. Suppose for a minute our eyes could perceive all the different colours and energy that surrounds us every day. Imagine you could see every living being's aura. Imagine you could see how they interact with each other. Imagine if you could see how sound interacted with your aura.

Now let's imagine you could also see spirits' or people's guides. You could see Angels and other beings that coincide on the same realm. We want to believe these beings exist, but because we can't see them, we tend to not believe. The same applies for Nature Spirits, call them what you may - Faery, Fae, Elementals, Devas. They are known by many names around the world. We want to believe in these too, but again, we need to see them to believe them. I too was on the fence with this one for so long, but I am no longer. These beings do indeed exist, however, because Humans have romanticised the images of these beings over time, they seem to just be a fairy tale for most. For me, I do not see faeries wearing leaf skirts and wings flying around my back yard. I sense them, like a whisper most times. Dancing around the edges of my perception. It's like Nature itself is trying to talk to me. It wasn't until I really deconstructed my view of the universe and human nature that I completely sensed their presence. Being pure of heart and intent with a genuine care for the earth, nature and humanity, along with being extremely sensitive, has given me the ability to make a connection. And this is helped through the use of crystals. Quartz can help amplify energy, so if you want to communicate with a whisper, that's a great place to start.

What I have come to realise is that Nature Spirits, Faeries, Angels, Devas and Elementals are all very real. They are all intelligent beings and they all have a soul purpose, just like us. Many are here to help humanity in our experience with Guides and Angels. Nature Spirits, Fae, Devas and Elementals are the same but they generally work with the purpose of ensuring life on the planet through Nature. They guide

Artwork credit - Nicola McIntosh © 2014

Nicola McIntosh

things to grow and occasionally their Soul Purposes cross paths with Humans. This is going to start happening more and more. They are now sensing that Humanity is starting to reach a point where something needs to be done and all these energies are converging on us to help steer us back onto a path of working together and living as one with the Earth. They are realising that many of us are awake now and aware of what is happening, and they are reaching out to us so we can spread this message.

How can we claim to be intelligent beings when we are the ones not living on this earth in harmony with the environment and every other living being? Look at a forest and see how the tree roots grow around the rocks, see how the running creek flows around whatever lies in its path. We need to start learning how to adapt, how to change our way of thinking and living on this earth. We need to deconstruct our beliefs and take a good look at if they now fit in this new age. It's time to look inside yourself and feel what your soul purpose is. It's time to now start living your authentic self and help with the changes that are happening on the earth. Look at how you can live more sustainably, welcome the Fae and Elementals into your life.

> Look at how you examine the world. Look at everything in Nature as though it is a living being and give it the respect you would another person. Everything has an intelligence and a soul purpose.

CRYSTAL Q&A

What are faery crystals?

There are a handful of beautiful crystals and stones that are associated with Faeries. If you are wanting to become more in tune with their energy, this is a great way to start.

Staurolite - I was amazed at how powerful this stone is. The cross is naturally formed and I feel it represents the 4 elements. You will indeed become more aware of the elementals using this stone. It will help you to ground and work from the heart, the perfect combination when working with this energy.

Chiastolite - A very similar stone to Staurolite, in that it also has a cross. This cross is very representative of the Medicine Wheel. It is a very earth-based stone and is a very protective stone when worn. Again, another good stone to connect to the elementals of the four directions.

Fairy Quartz - A beautiful crystal to help connect you with the Faery Kingdom. A very sparkly stone, which reminds us of sparkly Faery energy. Covered in tiny little crystals around the central larger one, it helps with collective energy work. Like its larger variety, Spirit Quartz, it is also a high vibration stone that radiates its energy in all directions, whilst the main crystal still focuses its energy in one direction.

If you have a crystal question you would like answered in our next issue, please email Nicola directly at: nicola@spiritstone.com.au. (Please keep in mind that not every question may be able to be answered in each edition).

Nicola is an artist with a passion for Nature & Crystals, who is currently studying Celtic Shamanism. Her aim is to help empower others through her work, to bring about healing.

Contact Nicola at: www.spiritstone.com.au

1. Focus on what inspires you most.

2. Follow the flow. When you're not blocked you're following your purpose.

Your top 5 tips to discover one's soul Purpose in Life

with Gabrielle Bernstein
New York Times bestselling author of Miracles Now, and May Cause Miracles.

3. Don't look for your purpose. Instead, release all that blocks you from it.

4. Be in joy. When you focus on what is joyful you create a connection to your inner spirit. This spirit is what allows your purpose to shine through.

5. Honor your truth

Gabrielle Bernstein has been named "a next-generation thought leader" by Oprah Winfrey and has been named "a new role model" by The New York Times. She is the New York Times bestselling author of Miracles Now, and May Cause Miracles. Her two additional titles include of Add More ~ing to Your Life and Spirit Junkie. Gabrielle is also the founder of HerFuture.com, a social networking site for women to inspire, empower and connect.

Presented by Earth Events, Gabrielle will be visiting Sydney, Melbourne and Brisbane with her Spirit June Australia Tour in January 2015.

Visit here for information and tickets
http://earthevents.com.au/gbtix/

The Inherent Soul Agreement

What happens when one discovers the essence of their true Soul purpose? Gem Green reveals how this led to a time of Soul searching and discovery.

My friends at inSpirit, Kerrie and Nicolle, have often said that when they choose a theme for an upcoming edition of the magazine, they live it, they breathe it, it becomes an integral part of their lives until the edition is complete. Well, this theme, that of the SOUL, has gripped me like none other before it. It has left me raw, turned me upside down and inside out.

Yet it has also opened a new level of awareness, offered me new eyes, greater love and compassion and a whole new set of questions to be contemplated and realised regarding our inherent soul agreements. I share this gift of personal insight with you in the hope that it assists you in your journey to discovering and/or accepting (or changing) your inherent soul agreement.

Inherent: '...in the nature of something though not readily apparent.'

It is challenging to discover one's true soul purpose as agreed upon before we were even a breath in our mother's womb. Challenging it is to really discover that which we were born to carry out upon this earthly plain. Challenging to sift through the pride or the negative input of our ego self to reveal the true, authentic soul purpose of our existence. What can be even more challenging at times is to accept our inherent soul agreement with love, compassion, even courage and commitment if need be, when we discover this deep and meaningful truth that is the very reason our soul self-chose to live in this lifetime, this realm.

Yet the inherent soul agreement, the soul's main purpose for journeying on this plane is and always has been, one of the main aspects of what we as spiritual beings strive to achieve, to recognise or to become aware of during our magickal journeys here on earth. And, once we become fully aware of our reason for being here, it is our birth right to live according to our inherent soul agreement……or is it?

As a goddess of water, born of sea and of foam, I believe nothing less than our inherent soul purpose had already been agreed upon well before our soul took its first breath upon this earthly plane. Yet now I find myself pondering, what of the validity of staying true to the path that I, as my soul self, agreed upon many moons ago?

With a greater awareness of my own soul agreement and of how we each intertwine with the soul agreements of ALL those that are close, near and dear to us, is even questioning the validity allowed? My soul's agreement and the choices that I make, whether that be in a detached state or through my ego self, has cause and effect on the soul agreements of those around me and even those that I do not know yet. This is to say that my choices can disrupt, deter or delay someone else's journey! Really? And if this is the case, should I even be questioning my soul? Should I even be thinking of myself ahead of my partner or my children for example?

I once thought that if only I knew my intended purpose I would easily follow it with a dedication of knowing that I walked true. Now that I have that awareness, I no longer believe that it is always easy to walk your intended path even if you have the map and a complete knowing. In actual fact, and thanks to my ego self, for me, it has raised more questions, it has awakened more contemplation and time for meditation!

So with my new found clarity, I lay out the blueprint and wash over it with a wave of perspective and I ask "How can I not follow the soul's map if others' journeys depend or rely upon it as per their own agreements? Do I have the right, me in my meagre existence, not to follow my own soul agreement? Even if it is because I want to experience more love and more joy? If we are consciously aware of our true authentic soul agreement, our true purpose, are we then able to change it? And should we even consider changing it?" With each question comes contemplation, and more questions and more soulful contemplation. Always remain true to the fact that the answers you seek, although they may be to the same questions, are your personal and soulful truth to live by.

Gem embraces the energetic power of seashells, sea animals and the waters of ocean and sea every day, connecting and creating with this amazing and unique energy to enhance and guide not only her magickal life journey but yours as well if you allow it. "May The Magick & Wisdom of Ocean & Sea's Inspire Us All" www.gemgreen.com.au

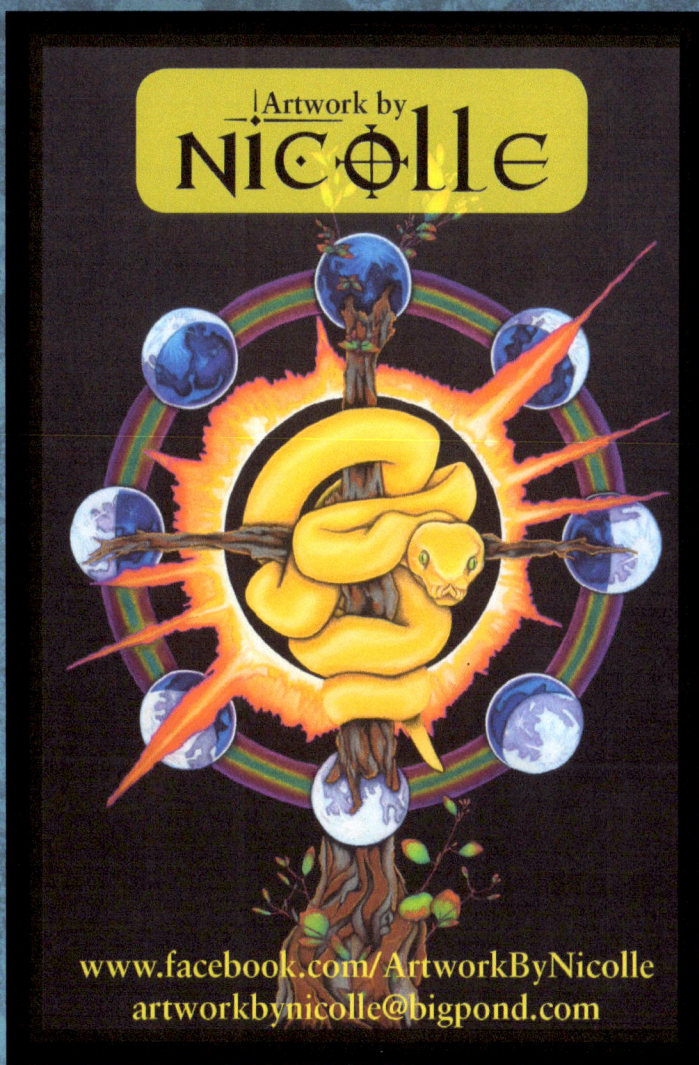

Seeking a Magical Name

"CALL MY NAME!" cried the childlike Empress with tears in her eyes as her ivory tower crumbled all around her. All Bastian needed to do was give the Empress a new name to save her and her land Fantasia! From one of my all time favourite movies "The Never Ending Story" the power of a magical name became known to me. I was very young when I first saw this movie, but even then I felt the power of that scene. It was so inspiring to me and I would often daydream wondering what I would call that Empress if I were given the opportunity. I dreamt up a fantastical name and I kept it for my young self for many years - but that was not MY story……

"Since human beings have believed in spirit we have named it. By naming this divinity we honour it, and by naming the divinity within ourselves we do the same." ~ Natasha Heard.

My name was Natasha Riedl back then, my father's last name. I never knew him very well - my mother re-married, so I was a Riedl in a family of Smiths as I grew up, a little lost and unsure of where I fit in. When I married my magic man, my last name changed to Heard, we had a family and I finally felt I had my own little tribe - they call me Flower! My daughter first called herself Butterfly when she was young and I was her Flower - it stuck! I feel this is a very special name that the ones I love the most know me by. Then when I started my business 'Blessed Branches' and could see my name Natasha Heard associated with magical tools and natural witchery, I felt like it finally fit me! The energy of my name evolved as my magic and creativity grew.

Now in my 30's, magic is no fantasy to me anymore. Magical energy flows through every aspect of my adult life and it resides deep within my bones. My soul knows magic from past lives I have lived as a witch and a healer and a magical tool maker. My soul is the same but my names have changed, and now in this life I have been gifted a new magical name by the Goddess! I have been through a few tough lessons to grow into the energy and power of this name. I have had to accept all that I am and have seen the darker side of myself before being bestowed with the honour of this new name. Now I have it I will keep it a secret within my soul to be shared only within the divine realms of magic.

SO, WHAT IS A MAGICAL NAME? A magical name is a sacred name you give to yourself or can be gifted to you by spirit. It is unique to each person, reflecting your heart, your soul and your mystique. With a magical name you can leave your regular persona for a while and become your sacred self. The name should give you confidence and empower you in your connecting, crafting and magical weaving. It will bring you one step closer to the divine, to your higher self and closer to the Gods and the Goddess, making it easier to commune with spirit! Giving yourself a magical name gives you a power boost within the realms of magic where you can cast and weave cosmic energy, becoming one with the past, present and future, manifesting your dreams and desires and bringing those energies into your everyday life. When you have finished your magical workings you take back your regular name and everyday personality. It is an enchanting way to step into and out of the magical realms.

CAN I CHOOSE MY OWN MAGICAL NAME? You can choose a magical name, YES! You can! Any name that feels right can be taken and you do not have to ask permission from anyone else (although I would be cautious of naming myself after a God or Goddess without asking the divine first). The way you spell your name and the way it is pronounced is also your choice. Some may choose a name in the beginning of their spiritual journey and then later on change it to something that suits their magical style a little more. Others will wait until they have studied the craft for a year and a day before taking a magical name. Some may take it at the time of initiation. It all comes down to your personal choice as individual as your magical ways and workings. You can choose your name from anything that inspires magic within you, a spirit creature teacher such as the Wolf or Raven, a colour or crystal that is special to you such as Silver or Amethyst, a time of day or year such as Twilight or Winter - anything naturally beautiful and connected to magic FOR YOU! You could of course combine these special things to create your own individual, Magical Name.

Another way to gain a magical name is to ask or to be gifted a name by the Goddess or by the Gods. It may come from your spirit guides or your higher self - perhaps even the faeries or angels may gift you a magical name. You could go on a journeying mediation where you meet a guide who gives you a name, or perhaps a dream will show you your magical name written above an ancient doorway - it is all very personal how you choose or how you may be gifted this magical name.

CAN I SHARE MY MAGICAL NAME WITH OTHERS? You can, but beware who you share your sacred name with! Only those you feel 100% safe with should be entrusted with your magical name as it could be used against you - think Rumplestiltskin! Some pagans have a name that can be shared with magical folk and friends for open rituals and ceremonies, then they also have a secret name they keep to themselves for personal power and spiritual connection.

Whatever you end up naming your magical self, be sure it gives you strength and courage, it should be positive and empower YOU! It should resonate within your heart, your spirit and sit peacefully within your bones. When that name is presented to you a feeling of ancient being will wash over you from many lifetimes resonating as one and when it is whispered back to you by the Goddess you will know - it is perfectly yours.

With Love and Magical Blessings ~ Natasha xx

Natasha Heard is a creatress of all things magical! A natural witch ~ her magical life and connection to the Earth flow into all her creations. Specialising in Wands, Sceptres and Staves; and creating with her horticulturalist husband Michael, Blessed Rune sets and Tree of Life Bind Rune Talismans. Her innate connection with all aspects of the natural world and passion for magic is what makes her a true creatress of powerful, magical tools.

Natasha can be contacted Email: blessedbranches@gmail.com or Facebook: Blessed Branches...magical tools by Natasha Heard.

GODDESS INSPIRATION

The Goddess and her many names

The Great Goddess has many faces, many names. Looking through history, reading different countries' mythologies and stories, we can see patterns in the energies and influences each Goddess rules over. The names may differ but they have an essence to them that is the same, a shining face of the Goddess. These divine deities have different personalities and life lessons to teach and share with us, and we may call upon their mystical energies to aid us when practicing magic. Spell casting for magical manifestation may require different aspects of the goddess to be called upon.

For Love - *Call upon the Roman Goddess Venus, or the Greek Goddess Aphrodite, Goddesses of love and beauty to aid you in attracting love.*

For Prosperity - *Call on the Hindu Goddess Lakshmi from whose palms rain golden coins, or the Roman Goddess Abundantia (aka Lady Luck), who carries her cornucopia of abundance.*

For Fertility - *Call upon the Greek Mother Goddess Demeter, or the Norse Goddess of Spring and new life Ostara.*

For all things Magical – *Hecate, the mystical Greek Goddess of magic and witchcraft will guide your wand, or the Celtic Morrigan for all craft workings.*

For Protection - *Call on the Hindu White Tara for gentle protection, or the Egyptian Goddess Isis who will shield you with her mighty golden wings.*

If ever in doubt, simply call for the Goddess and graciously ask she guide you under whatever name she likes! After all, the Goddesses and her many names are simply faces of the divine energy that will aid and guide you whenever magical assistance is needed.

Picture Credit: Samsahra Lee Contact: bohindia@hotmail.com

SPIRITED ANIMALIA

with Animal Dreaming's Scott Alexander King

Hi Scott. The other night my husband dreamt he had a White Tiger and cubs sitting on him in our backyard. They were holding antennas! The same night, I dreamt he had a Panda standing beside him as he lay sleeping in bed, and the Panda was operating on him! (Yep, just like surgery). I thought it really interesting that we both had animal dreams about him on the same night. Any thoughts? Cheers and blessings to you. Natalie M

Hey Natalie. In my world, the White Tiger is a symbol of submissive, protective, feminine power. It is also energetically ruled by the introspective energies of the West, and the reflective qualities of autumn. During autumn, everything is preparing itself for a time of Deep Rest. The leaves turn to shades of red, auburn and gold before falling from the tree, leaving it exposed to the harshness of winter. For some, winter heralds the coming of snow, when the earth slips into dormancy and the animals into hibernation. Many animals slip into a state of Deep Rest every now and then. We sometimes call this hibernation. The animals embrace their times of Deep Rest, and actually look forward to it. We used to embrace our periods of Deep Rest too, but over time we began to hear Deep Rest as Dee-Pressed (depressed).

What the animals know to be true (a truth we have long forgotten) is that when we feel the need to go within, like the Bear going into her cave, we need to surrender to the need. We need to do NOTHING during this period of time except be still, quiet and submissive; to place our head on Great Spirit's chest and REST, listen to the steady beat of the Earth Mother's heart. When we find ourselves facing the void space of 'Deep Rest', we can very easily slip into despair and panic. I believe your husband has been experiencing a time of overwhelming grief and what may be described as 'depression'.

White Tiger has come because he's yearning for stillness, rest and quiet; a personal (though brief) time of winter-like dormancy. He's being told that when he feels like the sun's gone down and that it may never rise again, just be still, sit quietly and sleep. Hibernate, like the Bear might. Rest. Be still. Because, after a while, the sun will rise once again, the darkness will be banished and he will shine once again. He needs to remember that after night, the dawn always breaks and the sun returns,

bringing with it clarity, direction and energy to take on the world. Deep Rest: it's like sleep, only you're awake to witness it.

In your husband's case, Natalie, the hibernating Bear manifested as the Panda - an animal that 'cries for the people'. It's an animal that mourns times past, expresses sorrow for things lost and grieves things long forgotten – hence the dark tear stains around each eye, and it's blemished paws caused by rubbing the eyes free of those tears. It's an animal that invite us to 'cut through' the manifested beliefs that keep us locked in a world of mundane practicalities, and invites us to cry, scream and express our wants, dreams and desires without fear of ridicule or of being muzzled. I think your husband is grieving Natalie; grieving for a lost opportunity, a lost childhood or a lost dream that may have been realised and brought to fruition if life had taken a slightly different course for him growing up.

I suspect the Tiger cubs (holding antenna) represent your husband's heart-yearning to be heard, noticed and acknowledged, to reclaim the power he felt or dreamed of during his youth, and to realise the dream of not being submissive any longer, but to roar from a very ancient place and to be heard. I truly believe the dreams both you and your husband witnessed were indicating the soon-to-be-realised beginnings of his 'Soul Purpose'; why he is 'here' as opposed to what he's physically doing to make good in the world. I think your husband is soon to wake up from a very long sleep, Natalie - and when he does, his life will totally change for the better (not to mention yours and your family unit as a whole). Good luck. And please, keep me informed.

Scott Alexander King is a shaman, visionary and Zoomancer – an individual that examines the habits and appearance of animals to help explain or reveal the future path of other people. He is the author of, among others, 'World Animal Dreaming', a shamanic field guide that offers insight into the wisdom of over 300 exotic and native Australian animals published by Animal Dreaming Publishing. Scott is available for interviews, workshops and seminars. To learn more about Scott and his work, go to: www.animaldreaming.com or connect with him and his animals on Facebook www.facebook.com/scottalexanderking / www.facebook.com/animaldreamingsanctuary

Photo credit: Karen Branchflower

Cosmic Codes
with Amanda Coppa

Moon Magic for the months ahead.

The moon represents our emotions, feelings, femininity, intuition and unconscious. Every month the moon waxes and wanes in regular cycles. Paying attention to the moon cycles allows us to work with its energy rather than against it. During every month we have both a new moon (new beginnings) and full moon (release & closure) which supports us in establishing new patterns whilst clearing outdated ones from our life.

OCTOBER 2014

8:51pm AEST Wednesday 8

With a full moon lunar eclipse in Aries, the sign of the warrior, we can expect strong and dynamic energies. We feel energetic and enthusiastic but are more likely to be impulsive, reckless and impatient at this time too. Emotional upsets can arise more easily but hot heads will only get us into a mess. The fiery energy of Aries can propel us forward, so we must channel this energy effectively into self-improvement, giving our projects a well needed boost or working cohesively with others.

Tip for Aries: You have the strength and stamina to move mountains.

7:57am AEST Friday 24

A new moon partial solar eclipse in the deep and mysterious sign of Scorpio adds potency to an already intense moon phase. Eclipses bring about some sort of 'personal crisis' that ultimately leads to positive change. New energy patterns are awakened and it's time to break free from limitations, self-sabotage or anything that holds us back. We need to pay attention to doors that are now opening for us and trust that with self-confidence, courage and determination anything is possible!

Tip for Scorpios: Self-reflection will help you find the best direction to take.

NOVEMBER 2014

8:23am AEST Tuesday 7

The full moon in the earthy and sensual sign of Taurus illuminates the skills, resources, passion and creative talents we have at our disposal. Ruled by the planet Venus, we are reminded to let love be our guide as we consciously focus on that which brings us stability, comfort, pleasure and contentment. Our intentions are mighty important right now and this full moon will see us entering a cycle of creation, stability and feeling comfortable in our skin. Finding balance and holding strong in this new vibrational space will be very liberating if we allow it.

Tip for Taureans: Spend time in nature to release the old and recharge your batteries.

10:33pm AEST Saturday 22

With the new moon in the philosophical and expansive sign of Sagittarius, it's a powerful cycle of manifestation and new beginnings. Now is the time to dig your ground, plant your seeds and patiently wait for them to bloom. The manifestation process is quite simple - you have an idea, then that idea meets with a feeling. When that feeling is loving and aligned with truth it creates a seed of manifestation. As you focus, nourish and take inspired action, that seed begins to grow and blossom. Use the energy of this moon to connect you with your highest potential.

Tip for Sagittarians: Be honest with yourself in all of your activities and actions.

DECEMBER 2014

10:27pm AEST Saturday 6

The full moon in the expressive sign of Gemini places greater importance on balancing our deeper emotions and thoughts. Thoughts are like magnets - instantly attracting and manifesting your future. Now is the time to broaden your perspective and gently release old thought or communication patterns that no longer serve you. The full moon illuminates the importance of staying focused in the now and being aware of the signs, synchronicities and messages all around. If you are feeling anxious, unsettled or stressed use the power of your breath to rapidly release, refocus and realign your energy patterns.

Tip for Gemini's: Speak your truth from the heart.

11:36am AEST Monday 22

With the new moon in the earthy and practical sign of Capricorn, it's time to knuckle down and get serious about your plans and goals. Holding a clear vision of that which you are working towards and committing to the task at hand will prevent you from spreading yourself too thin. Luck and abundance comes from what you initiate now. It's an optimal time for you to simplify things and make life easier. Listen to your thoughts, words and feelings.

Tip for Capricorns: If you can dream it you can do it.

Amanda Coppa is a heart-centred crystal healer who incorporates astrology, numerology, Reiki and oracle cards into her work. She is passionate about self-healing, empowerment and helping you understand the REAL you.

Connect with Amanda at http://www.facebook.com/cosmiccodes.

Because We All Agreed

Rita Maher delves into the world of young hearts and as the adults in their world, how important and formative the care of their hearts you offer can be…

When we are gifted our children we often do not question why they have come into our life. Most of us plan our families, so we inherently believe that we have chosen the right time for them and therefore we are in control of this. Nothing could be further from the truth. These choice were often made long ago, as our souls forged contracts with others. Most times before we even incarnated. We have all chosen to learn and expand during our human existence, and we choose those in our soul group who are able to help in the process to be a part of our lives whilst here. For some of us this presents as challenges, for others it's about who can help us reach our destiny, who is able to nurture our learning in the best way possible.

My understanding of the soul contract was brought to light by my son who was 3 years old at the time. Whilst on a family day out driving to Minnamurra Falls, he asked "Remember when you and dad where driving down this road and I chose you to be my family?" In a stunned reply, I asked "When?" To that he replied "Before I was born I chose you." I can say without doubt that this small conversation changed my view on how our children come to be with us.

A year later he knew my second child's name even before I was 5 months pregnant. He told me one day that when Sebastian called me mum, I would explain that I was his mum first. When quizzed on who Sebastian was, he replied "My brother in your tummy". When I asked about the name, he said his brother had told him it. So our children's siblings make agreements with each other as well as with us.

Now it's all very well to say we all had a nice little agreement up there and we are here to learn, grow, support, expand and understand each other. BUT! Most of us are not conscious of what our agreement was, so how will that help us now? Firstly you don't need to be conscious of what was in the agreement. Yes, you read correctly - you don't need to know! If you were told your agreement was to have a child that would always argue with you, never do what they are told, be a nightmare all through their first 15 years of life, not allow you to get more than a couple of hours sleep a night and struggle at school, how many of you would raise your hand and say "Yes I will have that one?" Exactly! You don't need to know the agreement. Our soul knows it and that's what matters - not what our conscious mind thinks.

You also need to know this - you have free will in life once you incarnate, so you make or break that soul contract. You may change direction in life and therefor no longer be the best person for that child to incarnate with. So again you don't need to know why you agreed.

In saying that, it doesn't mean that we cannot gain understanding of how to work with each other for the betterment of our soul's lesson. Have you ever stopped and actually really observed the dynamics of your family, and asked the questions "What are we all learning from each other?" "What am I teaching?" "What are they learning?" and vice versa. While we all think that the first born is the natural leader, it's not always the case. The middle child does not always get forgotten and the youngest is not always the baby. For those who are pregnant, sit and meditate and connect in with this little one's soul, ask the question "Why are we together and how can we help each other?"

Look at the interests of your children then look at the interests of your own childhood. Do they have a similar quality? Has your child reawakened in you something you have long ago forgotten? Explore how your child has taught you things about being a parent. How do your children interact with their siblings, what are they learning from each other? Ask yourself how you can enhance the family. When you stop and listen and observe, so much more is revealed to you. Watch your children because they are observing the family as well. They are more connected then you imagine. Have the conversation with your child "Why did you chose me as your parent?" The answer may shock you and even awaken you.

The question is not really why we are all together - it is "How can we get the best out of being together?" For all of us, you can be sure of this: Our children are the greatest blessing we can ever hope for - challenges, hiccups, warts and all. They are the greatest teachers in how to rise to the occasion of being a parent. Together we are all each other's best students as we travel and expand our understanding of life.

Rita Maher is a Psychic Medium, Intuitive Counsellor and qualified Reiki Healer who has a passion for working with children and families. She specialises in meditation and intuitive guidance to help not just children but adults understand direction and change in their life, helping create secure environments for young minds to grow and thrive.

Soul Purpose Salad

Savor Your Food, Savor Your Life
Eat Slow, Connect to Your Soul Purpose with MEADOW LINN

Food is much more than just food. It may seem surprising, but you really can eat your way to a deliciously enlightened life! When we think of a spiritual path, we often envision meditation, yoga, fasting, chanting, or prayer. We don't usually consider our everyday meals as a potential gateway to mystical transformation. Yet, the food you eat and your approach to it can be one of the most powerful pathways to spiritual renewal.

You incarnated onto this planet with a mission. There is indeed a reason you're here, and part of your journey while you're in this physical realm is to experience life to the fullest and to listen to the messages of your soul. In the dizzying pace of life, sometimes this can be a challenge. The average number of rings on a phone—before someone gets impatient and hangs up—is three rings! It's less than eight seconds, on average, before someone gets restless and moves on to the next thing. All the so-called timesaving devices—such as dishwashers, cars, cell phones, e-mail, and instant messaging—in fact, have not saved us time for leisure and relaxation; they've only sped up our frenetic pace. As the speed of life increases, we inevitably eat faster and faster. We dine on microwaved frozen pizza while sitting in front of a computer, talking on the phone, or watching television. As a consequence, we don't taste our food, and more important, we don't taste and savor our life. This approach to food diminishes our ability to fulfill our purpose to the deepest extent.

To connect even more intimately with your purpose in being here on earth, as a suggestion, spend time living in an unhurried manner. As you slow down, remarkable insights will wash over you. You'll be at the right place at the right time more often, and you'll also be in alignment with your soul purpose more often. When you cook or eat slowly and methodically, you're living in the present moment, rather than thinking about the things you've done in the past or the things you should be doing in the future. It's in these times when you're truly experiencing "now" that you're most open to hearing the truth of your soul.

Slow Down/Open to Spirit

- Look at the presentation of the meal. Embrace the colors, textures, and aromas. Relish in all of it!
- Take time to be grateful to the Creator and to those who grew the food, picked it, transported it, sold it, and prepared it. Every meal has a story to tell.
- Take the first bite. Put down your fork and slowly chew, savoring the nuances of flavor the way that you would savor a fine wine.
- Only after you've swallowed the first bite, take another. Be present and focused. Taste and smell the food.
- Remember to breathe deeply and relax as you eat.
- Allow more time for eating.
- As often as you can, eat without reading, watching television, working on the computer, texting, talking on the phone, or e-mailing. (We know it might sound really hard to do, but it's all part of the process of opening yourself to Spirit.)
- After the meal, spend a few moments being still before jumping up to do the dishes or put the food away. Quiet your mind, open your heart, and listen to the whispers of your soul.

Soul Purpose Salad

This is the perfect salad for slowing down and listening to the whispers from Spirit. Each delicious crunch of snap pea and vibrant burst of tomato will reveal an orchestra of flavor, texture, and sound. Quiet your mind. As you do this, you'll begin to take note of each individual ingredient and how they work together to form the whole. When you savor your meal, you'll be creating a template for savoring your life even more fully. And as you make a habit of eating in this way, your Soul Purpose will become clearer to you.

Serves 2-4
3 hardboiled eggs, peeled and cut
8 oz. snap peas, stringed, blanched, and cut into thirds
1 English (hothouse) cucumber, thinly sliced
8 oz. grape tomatoes, cut in half lengthwise
1 bunch of dill, roughly chopped
2 Tbsp. capers
¼ cup extra virgin olive oil
2 Tbsp. lemon juice
½ tsp. sea salt

To boil the eggs, place them in a small pan covered with at least an inch of cool water. Bring to a boil. 10-15 minutes of boiling is a good rule of thumb. Immediately plunge the eggs in cool water to stop the cooking. (To facilitate easy peeling, make sure the egg is wet when you peel it.)

Meanwhile bring another small pan of water to a boil. String the snap peas. To blanch the snap peas, put them in the boiling water for 1-2 minutes. Immediately drain and rinse with cool water. Slice them into halves or thirds (depending on their size) at an angle.

Meadow Linn is a writer and a chef, living in California with her dog, cats and chicken. She believes that living well and eating well should be tasty and fun. Meadow has just co-authored her first cookbook with Denise Linn which is available now through Amazon. **Contact Meadow at**: www.meadowlinn.com and www.savortheday.com

Birth Is The New Beginning

Through a sea of self doubt and fear, Claire brings herself to new strength and new beginnings.

Jude Garrecht eloquently unveils the inner most fears we all feeling when birthing a dream.

Claire looked out of her window at the clear night sky. It was a crisp night, with a hint of snow in the air. She stood there in the darkness with her arms wrapped tightly around her. A shiver ran down her spine. Not a cold shiver; more feelings of apprehension that filled her being. 'What if I can't handle this new beginning?' she quietly asked herself.

Claire had always been good at being a confidante to others. She always offered sound advice, encouraging them to take brave steps on life's journey. However when it came to taking her own advice, Claire fairly quivered in her boots. She lacked the most important ingredient of all when it came to taking a chance on life - self-confidence.

Claire reached down and placed a hand on her abdomen. She did this instinctively, not really knowing why. *'I know how much I want this'* she thought, *'but am I ready?'* How many times had she asked that same question of herself throughout her life?

The twinkling stars in the indigo sky grabbed Claire's attention as they seemed to grow brighter, but she shrugged off the thought as her over active imagination. *'Who am I kidding?'* she whispered. *'I am not capable; not good enough. I don't have the support I need.'* Her narrow shoulders slumped as she continued to look out her window. What was she waiting for, a sign that declared that she was ready; she was worthy? Did she want a neon billboard in the night sky that read *'Claire, go for it!'*? She giggled at the thought of her very own night time neon sign.

Her lip curled as she felt the old pangs of anxiety reach into the depths of her being. All she had ever wanted was to have something of her very own, something she had personally created. Claire was always there for others; a kind word of encouragement; helping others make their plans. Was it really her time to shine?

Claire felt that she had been preparing her whole life to give birth, and yet she still doubted that her preparations were enough. Would they ever be enough in her critical eyes? The stars twinkled brightly once more and Claire caught a glimmer of movement; then another and another. Flashes of intense light bombarded the night sky. The timing of this superb light show was not lost on her.

She stood there in awe at the magnificence of the meteor shower she was witnessing. Claire immediately understood the significance of the messages and the signs she was receiving throughout this timely evenT. This was indeed her own neon billboard and it was saying loud and clear 'Claire, go for it!'

Instinctively, both of her hands were now resting gently on her belly. She felt a warmth emanating from deep within her. Her inner fire was ignited. It had been lit long ago when she had first dreamt about an idea for helping humanity, a strategy for global change and peace for people everywhere.

She dreamt it; played with it and often shelved it with excuses of 'not the right time; I'm too busy; I will be RIDICULED; IT WON'T Work, who am I to think I could dream up a solution to certain global issues?'.

Claire had written and expanded her dream until this moment when doubt had again threatened to smother her with insatiable and numbing fear. Then a glorious shower of light had signalled a new birth; the birth of her long held dream. Light would always shine the way; she would always be supported. Claire knew she would never be alone. You see, in that shower of light, a reflection glowed in the window of her world. A reflection that showed a young woman and man; this woman and her young husband staring out of this same window – so long ago.

He, with his arms around her; hands on her pregnant belly; due to give birth any day. On that night, as they looked out at the night sky, a meteor shower had gifted them with a light show they had never before seen.

Claire was so much older now; her beautiful child grown; her husband had died long ago. And yet, in those few moments, standing at that window, witnessing the light, she felt his warm arms around her, his hands on her belly. She could hear his whispered words, that miracles happen and it was time to birth her dream. He would always be with her.

Humanity needed her to live her dream finally.

It was no longer fearful apprehension she felt deep within her. It had been replaced by anticipation and excitement. There was a big world outside that window and Claire had just glimpsed some of its awesome magic.

Jude Garrecht, author of 'From Grief to Goddess' book and Healing Cards, is passionate about helping others access their inner realms to write new chapters in their life story. Jude's intimate connection to Mother Earth and the messages that come from nature weave a path in the unity between mind, body, soul and emotions to form the foundations of her business 'Dreaming the Seed' and her formula for successful goal creation.

Jude is a Psycho Spiritual Hypnotherapist, a Colour Therapist and Clairvoyant. Contact Jude at: Web: www.dreamingtheseed.com & www.fromgrieftogoddess.com

SOUL SONG
with Laura Naomi

The soul naturally gravitates to what is calling. If a particular energy is appropriate for a soul's awakening, then this intuition will lead the soul into that space. Based on our gifts, our purpose is defined, and within this recognition lies the awakening and empowerment. In our society, it is most unusual to be nurtured into this awakening process. However, it is an integrated aspect of a shamanic or an earth-based society - to nourish the whole person, to integrate the spiritual and the physical worlds.

It came clear to me that there were two distinctive types of people as I spent time in very business-focused environments as a spirit-person. I saw there were a large percentage of those whose focus was primarily in the physical dimension - the body and materialistic where there is a severe lack of connection to soul and spirit. And then, a group, who I had already been aware of, of people who were predominantly focused on spirit and were not very present or connected to the physical world.

For me, I feel in both cases the secret for balance is the heart - because it's the doorway to both worlds and this is where you will find spirit and passion interwoven. The heart is nourishing both the spirit and the body. Passion is directly associated with what you love to do in the physical world and this is linked to spirit.

Another observation I've come across as a facilitator of healing, is that sometimes a soul's purpose is not in alignment with the body's purpose. If out of alignment, it causes physical problems (e.g. illness, sickness, dis-ease, etc.), or emotional imbalance (e.g. depression, apathy, loss of connection). Discovering the voice of the body is essential, and hearing what the body's purpose is in this life creates a symbiotic relationship with you as the soul. Part of your soul's purpose may be healing, however you may find that your body doesn't enjoy the way you are expressing this. If you continue expressing in a way that doesn't fully validate your body's purpose (way of being in the physical world), then this will eventually cause unhappiness and emotional imbalance. Perhaps your body feels happier healing via writing instead of healing sessions.

It's sometimes easy to get caught up in the pursuit of "advancement", enlightenment, wanting more recognition, more wealth, being the one, more possessions, prestige or more knowledge, etc. When we have fully embraced our soul's purpose and are embodying this physically, this frees up a lot of energy and ignites a deep happiness. We are in synchronicity with our physicality. This energy is incredibly powerful - you are so connected that magic happens.

Being in the energy of the heart, we are able to create the space needed in order to hear and connect with both soul and body purpose. As children we have this bond innately and often lose sight of this as we get older.

In a shamanic culture, when a child growth of the infant through adulthood. With guidance from the shaman, the child is observed and whatever he/she is naturally drawn to is carefully noted along with their abilities or gifts. The shaman will continue to aid and nurture the child (with the help of the community) in their gifts and the manifestation of this into the physical world. The shaman works with spirit guides and the medicine wheel in relation to the child's soul purpose to assist in their spiritual wellbeing. With this nurturing there is more of a balance and understanding between the spiritual and physical worlds, as opposed to our society where there is often a disconnect with this knowing.

In the Western world a lot of people are being drawn to shamanism in particular - as well as other spiritual paths - where there are opportunities to be initiated or reconnected to their soul purpose. Sometimes this reawakening process can take time because of the layers of unconsciousness that are hindering this knowing, yet in my own experience, it is always connected to the heart.

Your soul will always remind you, call you and move you, to live with fullness and wholeness, walking with magic and purpose in this life and beyond. All that is required is we answer the call.

Laura Naomi is a Contemporary Shaman, which blends the unique modalities of Zen practices, Shamanic and energy healing, space clearing and psychic and emotional counselling. She guides individuals, groups, corporations and businesses and is passionate about creating more awareness around energy and the spiritual world; how it affects us and how to harness this power to create a more harmonious lifestyle. - Contact Laura @ www.laura-naomi.com/ Phone: 1300 887 581

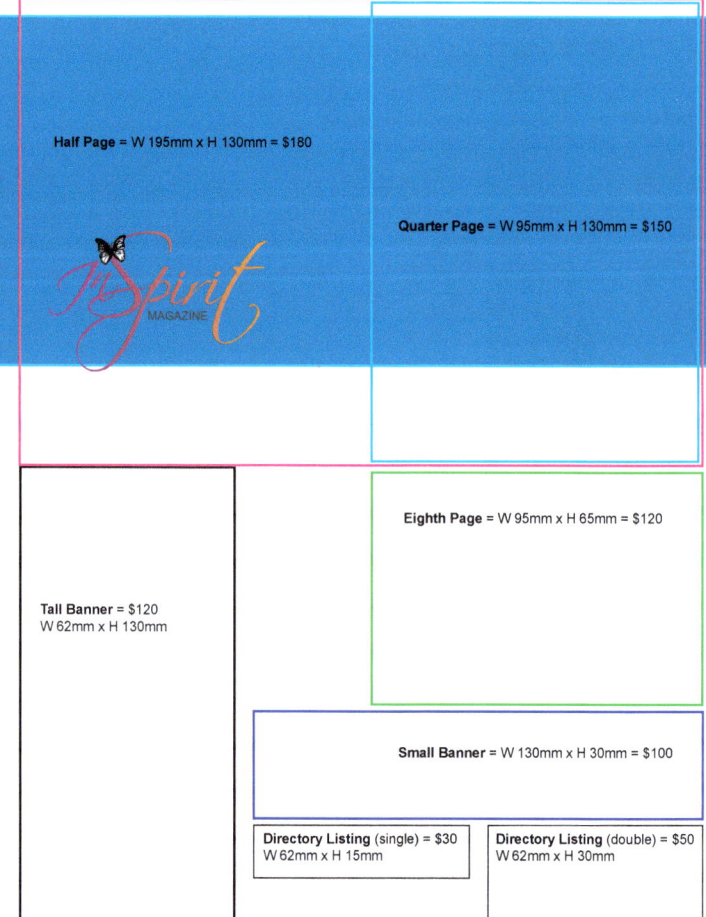

Advertise with Us

Advertise with inSpirit Magazine for :

- Best price value advertising,
- Your targeted market
- Cross promotion with Facebook and our email database

Contact us today at email: mail@inspiritpublishing.net

Full Page (Letter) = W 215mm x H 280mm = $210 / **Inside Front** or **Back Cover** = $240 / **Back Cover** = $270
(The full page ad has a 10mm margin which cannot have any writing in it, however the image may extend past the margin)

Half Page = W 195mm x H 130mm = $180

Quarter Page = W 95mm x H 130mm = $150

Tall Banner = $120
W 62mm x H 130mm

Eighth Page = W 95mm x H 65mm = $120

Small Banner = W 130mm x H 30mm = $100

Directory Listing (single) = $30
W 62mm x H 15mm

Directory Listing (double) = $50
W 62mm x H 30mm

inSPIRIT | review

Author: Serene Conneeley
Published: Blessed Bee Publishing

Serene Conneeley is an Australian author who has captivated many readers with the first two books of her current 'Into the Mists' trilogy series. Work on the third and final book will commence in November and be available for release in 2015.

INTO THE MISTS

Carlie, a vibrant teen on the cusp of womanhood and a bright future that she has mapped out for herself, loses all that she treasures in one tragic night.

She is then sent to the other side of the world to live with a relative she never knew existed and, in her mind, must be a terrible person.

As a reader, you connect deeply with Carlie as she struggles through her grief and tries to come to terms with her new life, so far removed from her old one. In her new life she finds herself stepping in two worlds - the present that is filled with grief, confusion and anger, where all that she thought is not as it seems; the other world is one of ancient magic of the land, where mysteries and secrets of the past are gradually revealed, offering healing and understanding if Carlie can accept them. The mystical energies have Carlie questioning her sanity, however these energies can show her a way through her despair and a chance for family connection and love again, if she chooses.

A captivating read that is nurturing and dramatic, with magic, mystery and ritual woven beautifully throughout.

INTO THE DARK

Put the kettle on and be ready for a sleepless night or two as the second book of this trilogy is hard to put down.

Carlie travels further into her world of self discovery and magic as she continues to come to terms with her grief and remapping her future. She is coming to realise she has found her spiritual home as she deepens her connections with her grandmother, her community and a newfound friendship continues to blossom as Carlie and her friend Rhiannon commit to exploring their magical paths together.

These relationships are challenged however, when Carlie finds herself drawn to love of a different kind - a love she is not ready to share and must keep secret. Frighteningly, a love that parallels echoes of the past, these same echoes that have ultimately defined her grief, present and future. A love that has Carlie making the most difficult choices of her life so far.

The choices that Carlie makes bring forth many twists and turns, more revelations about a past secret that so indelibly defines her life in the present, and a dramatic conclusion that has past and present colliding, leaving the reader reeling with shock, disbelief and wanting so much more.

AVAILABLE NOW
FOR DELIVERY IN NOV

Palmistry is an intuitive art and a highly accurate tool which gives you much insight about others and of course yourself.

Max Coppa's newest book, Love between the lines will provide you with the tools to find your own answers, assist you to recognise the signs and ultimately control the destiny of your love life.

www.inspiritpublishing.net

inSPIRIT | Directory

AROMATHERAPY

THE SCENTED LOTUS
Boutique Aromatherapy Store
www.thescentedlotus.com

ARTWORK

NICOLLE POLL
Artwork by Nicolle - Oracle Cards, Animal Magick Series, Soul Journey Portraits
E: artworkbynicolle@bigpond.com
FB: www.facebook.com/ArtworkByNicolle

NICOLA MCINTOSH
Graphic Design, Fairy & Fantasy Art, Oracle Cards & Writer
www.nicolamcintosh.com

ASTROLOGERS

DAVID WELLS
Teacher, Qabalist, Astrologer, Author & Past Life Therapist
www.davidwells.co.uk

CRYSTAL SHOPS

JOPO FENG SHUI & CRYSTALS
2 Revesby Road, Revesby NSW
T: +612 9785 0798

SPIRIT STONE
For crystals & new age supplies
www.spiritstone.com.au

MAGICAL TOOLS

NATASHA HEARD
Blessed Branches
www.blessedbranches.com

GEM~MER
Cryshell Magic
www.cryshellmagic.com.au

NUMEROLOGY

AMANDA COPPA
Crystal Healer, Numerology & Astrology
www.facebook.com/cosmiccodes

PERSONAL GROWTH

KYE CROW
Wunjo Crow – Sacred Clothing, Animal Sanctuary & Sacred Journey into the Animal Realm workshops
www.camelcampsanctuary.com
www.facebook.com/Wunjocrow

PSYCHICS & MEDIUMS

KERRIE WEARING
Author, Soul Coach & Medium
www.psychicmedium.com.au

RITA MAHER
Psychic Medium, Intuitive Counsellor and qualified Reiki Healer
www.steppingstones4life.com

SCIENCE & SPIRITUALITY

BRENDAN D. MURPHY
Author - The Grand Illusion
www.brendandmurphy.net

SHAMANISM

LAURA NAOMI
Consultations, Workshops & Seminars
www.laura-naomi.com

STORYTELLING & FOLKLORE

REILLY McCARRON
Faerie Bard, Folklorist & Storyteller with Harp
www.faeriebard.com
E: info@faeriebard.com
F: Faerie Bard

RADIO SHOWS

www.ghostsofoz.com

Would you like your listing included here? Email us at mail@inspiritpublishing.net for details.

Daily Soul Conversation Insight Cards

A moon inSpired 52 card deck featuring 22 inSight and affirmation cards and 30 Soul Conversation cards.
Wisdom of the Soul; Daily Soul Conversation inSight cards are a powerful companion for Soul Awareness.

with Kerrie Wearing

www.ingramcontent.com/pod-product-compliance
Lightning Source LLC
Chambersburg PA
CBHW041120300426
44112CB00002B/41